Josie and the Kite

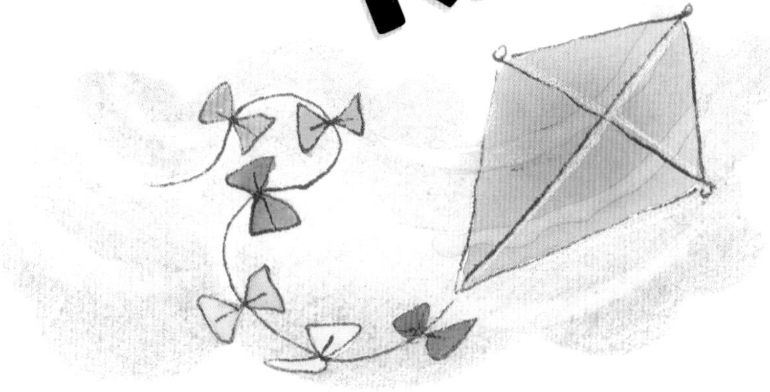

Monica Hughes
Illustrated by Lisa Smith

RIGBY

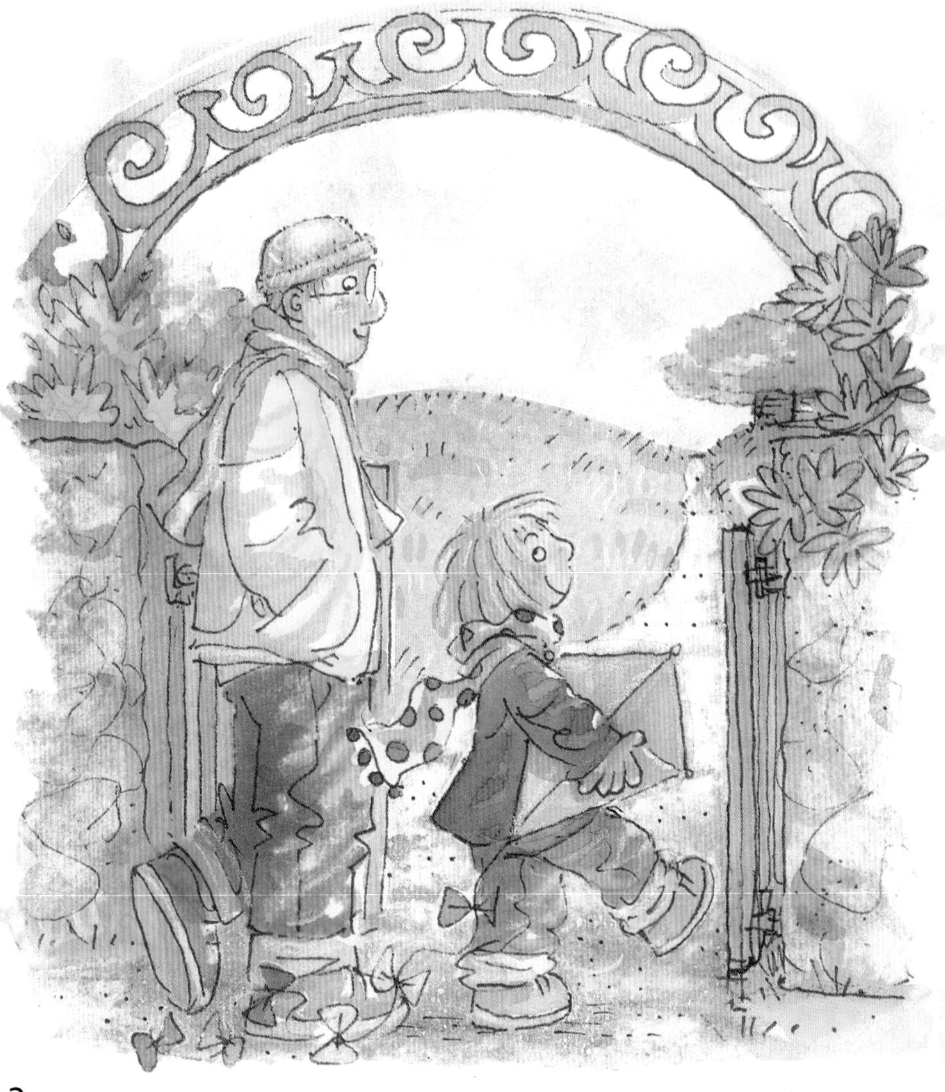

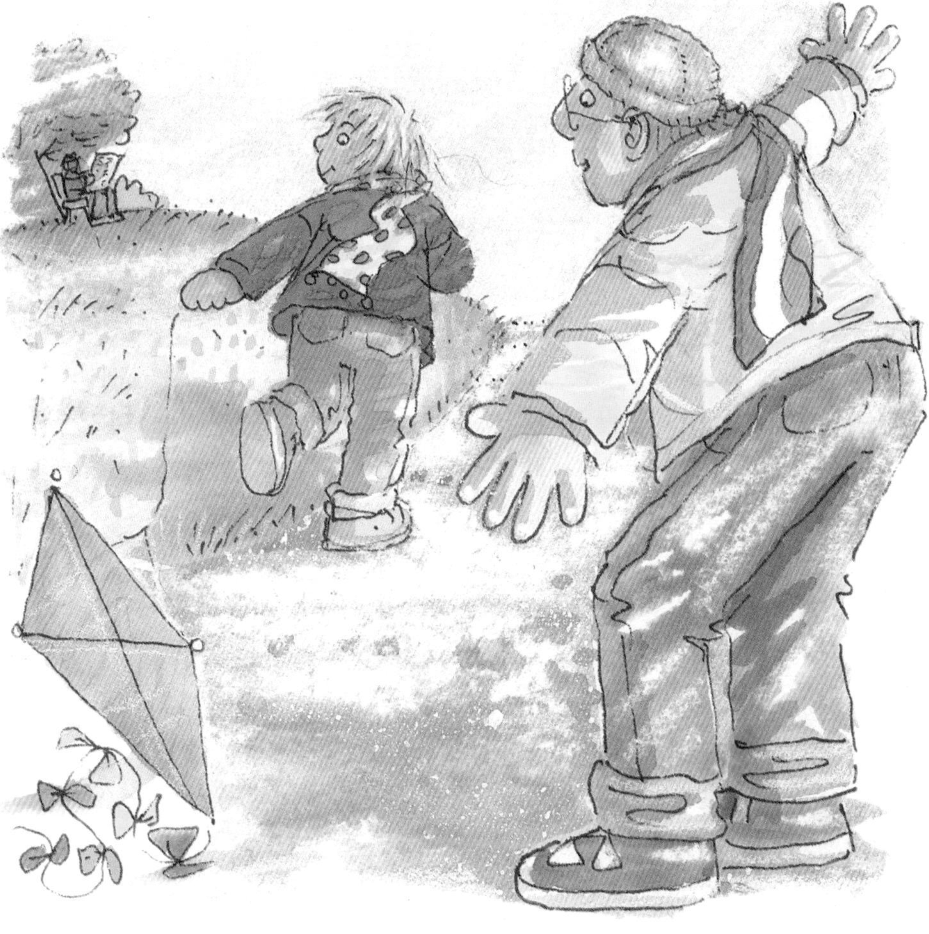

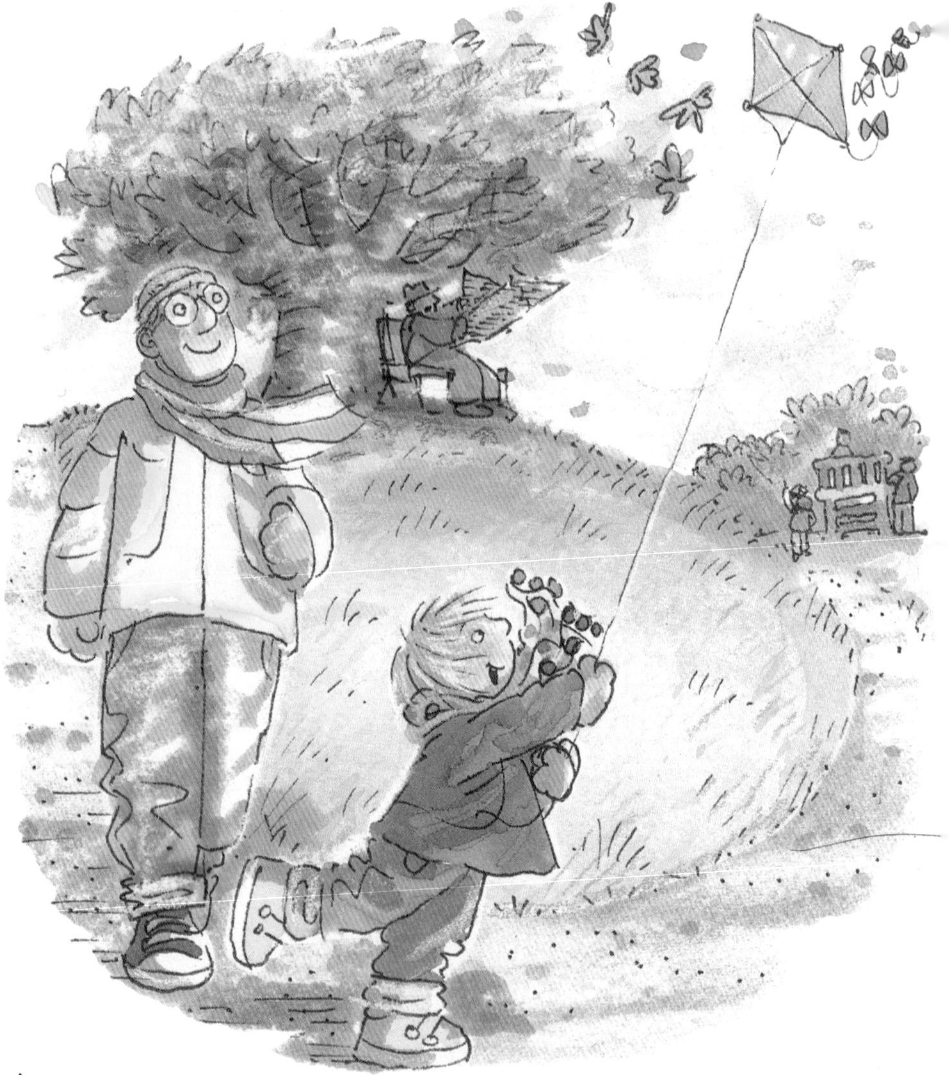

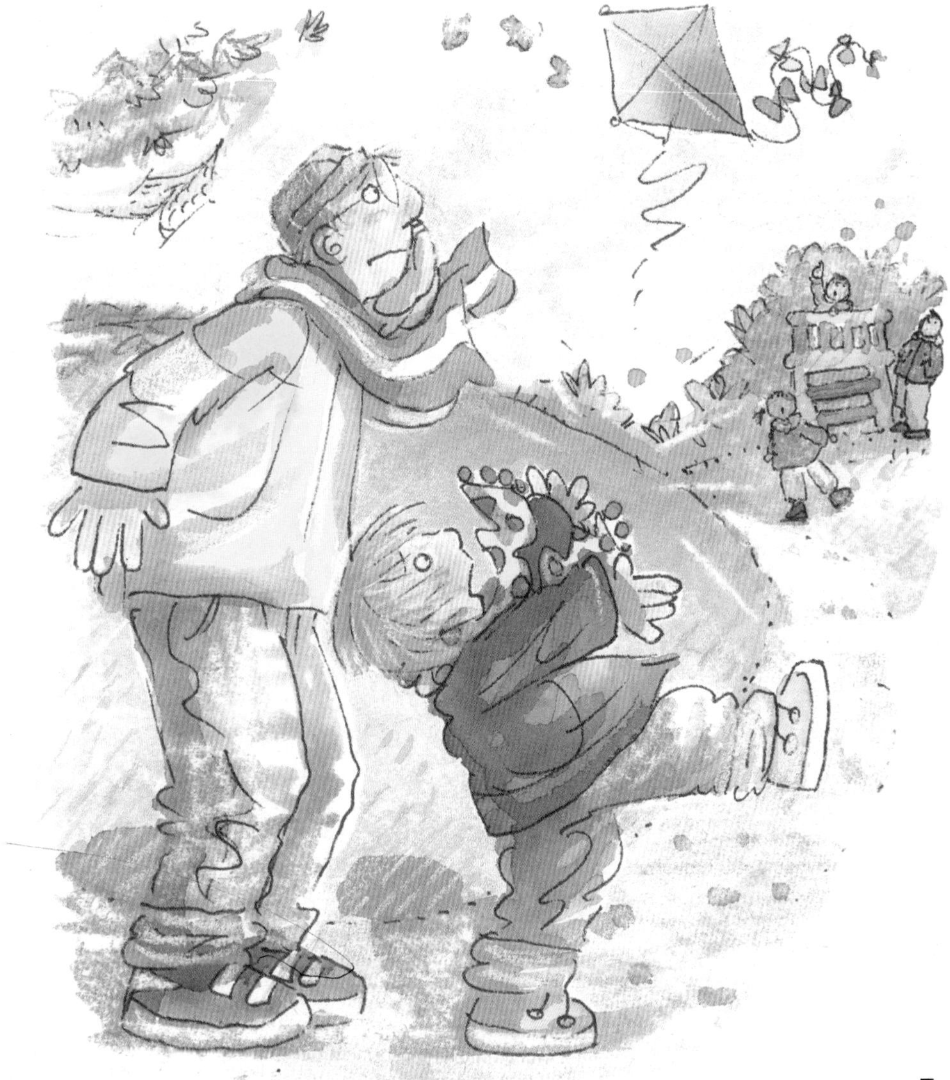

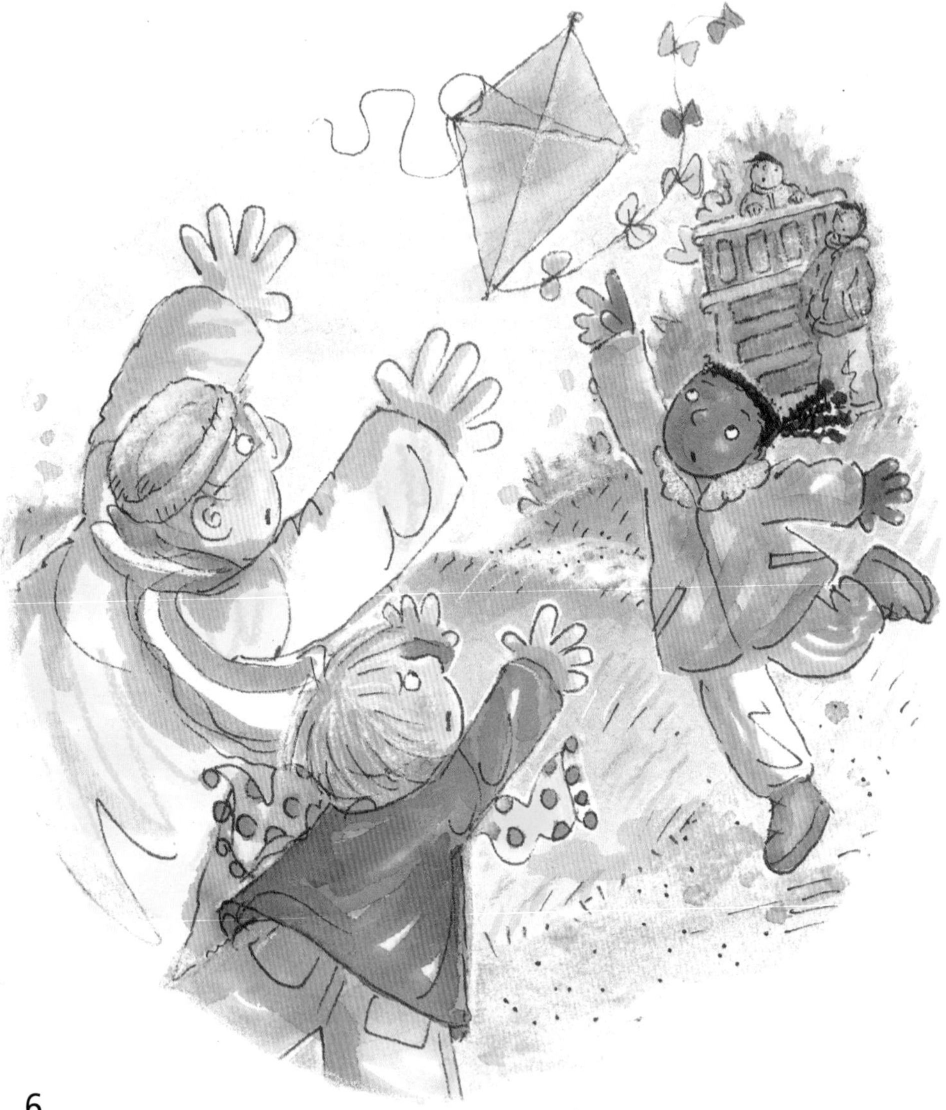

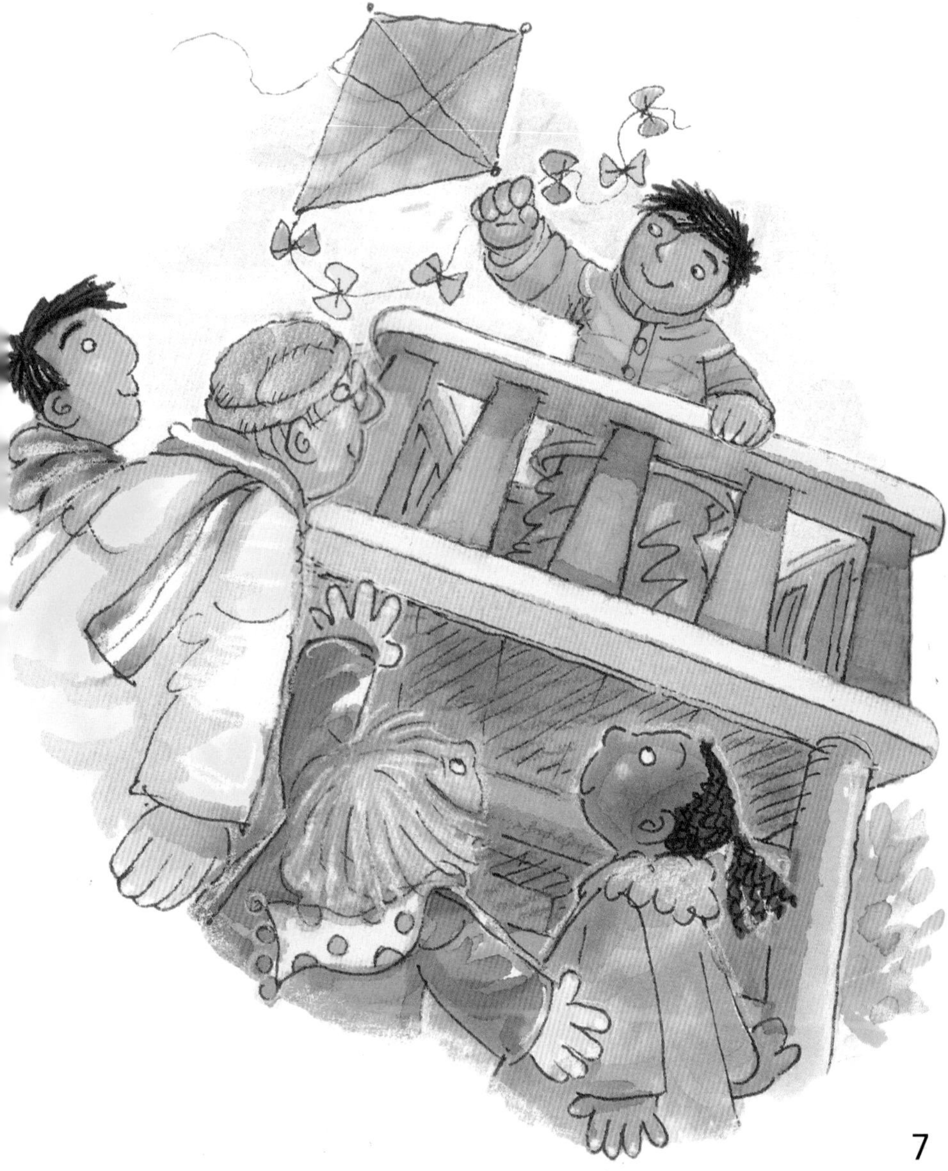

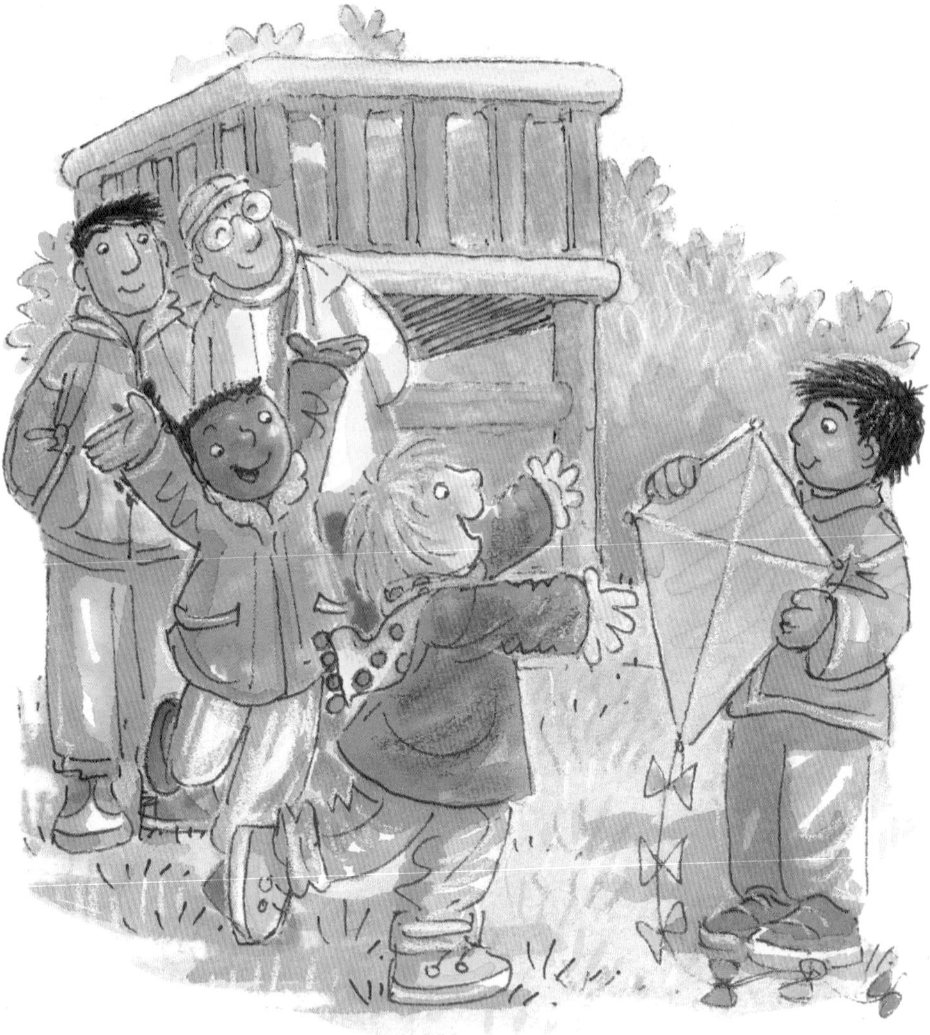